T0208040

The
Bumblebee
Is Not Supposed to Fly

It Defies All Odds.

Will You Defy the Odds
for Your Success?

The
Bumblebee
Is Not Supposed to Fly

Tyrone Ward

THE BUMBLEBEE IS NOT SUPPOSED TO FLY

Scripture quotations marked NIV are taken from the Holy
Bible, New International Version®. NIV®. Copyright ©
1973, 1978, 1984 by International Bible Society. Used by
permission of Zondervan. All rights reserved. [Biblica]

iUniverse books may be ordered through booksellers or by contacting:

iUniverse
1663 Liberty Drive
Bloomington, IN 47403
www.iuniverse.com
1-800-Authors (1-800-288-4677)

ISBN: 978-1-5320-6141-7 (sc)
ISBN: 978-1-5320-6142-4 (e)

Library of Congress Control Number: 2018912877

Print information available on the last page.

iUniverse rev. date: 11/05/2018

Contents

Preface

Our opportunities and our success in this lifetime here on earth are partly dependent on our thoughts, effort, attitude, foresight and actions. Success has different meanings to different cultures and races of people in the world. Success varies on a wide scale, even among a homogenous group of people.

For example, success for a man or woman living in a developing country may be locating a school in order to obtain a basic education. On the other hand, success for a person living in a developed country may be obtaining a bachelor's degree.

Therefore, when reading this book and being introduced to the various players, you will find that each person within these pages found success in different and diverse areas. Similarly, you have to find something that you want to accomplish, an area in which you have a burning desire to succeed. This will ultimately bring you the reward that you are longing for, but you have to be persistent and never quit!

Within the pages of this book, you will be introduced to some of the trailblazers who have helped humankind in the pursuit of happiness. This is a work in progress for the general public who are keen on reading and who may have some interest in reading this book.

To complete the undertaking of writing this book, I had to limit my research to two groups of people, namely, the black and white communities of the developed world.

This does not negate the contributions of other groups who have helped us along the path of development. Had I attempted to include all the people who contributed to the advancement of humankind, it would have been a daunting task.

It is my hope that when people of other cultures read this book, it will inspire them to write about others who have helped us in our development that has, so far, brought us from the Stone Age to allow us to enjoy our present accomplishments. In moving forward, governments must figure out how to move the 4 billion people who are stuck at the bottom of the economic pyramid up to a more desirable place in the pyramid.

Introduction

A job will give you a living,
but an idea, if acted upon, can make you a fortune
and quite possibly change the world, making it a
more peaceful place in which to live by providing
jobs and opportunities for the masses.

This book was written for you to use as a daily pocket guide. It is intended to help you move from where you are at present to any destination you may want to reach in life or toward any goal that you may want to achieve. It will show you that many others with fewer resources than you may have reached their potential and, in so doing, contributed to the growth and betterment of humankind.

Throughout the text, as you turn the pages, you will encounter the names of people who have taken *ideas* and changed them into *reality*, to move this world forward, making life better for millions of people who occupy this planet.

The Story of the Bumblebee

We are creatures of habit, and so is the bumblebee! We awake every morning and head out to our jobs because we have been conditioned to perform this task. On the other hand, the bumblebee flaps its wings and becomes airborne. But based on all scientific principles of flight, it is impossible for the bumblebee to fly. This is because its wingspan does not provide the boost that is required in order to give the lift that is necessary for the bumblebee to become airborne. Nevertheless, no one has told the bumblebee that it cannot fly, and it cannot understand the spoken word *can't*. As a result, it is not restricted in its thinking of *I can't*. Instead, it says "I can" and makes it happen.

To both substantiate and rebuff the argument with regard to the bumblebee, I will introduce you to what took place at a dinner table among a group of scientists and other professionals in Germany.

The account of this story first appeared in Germany in the 1930s. It is reported that one evening a group of scientists and other professionals were having dinner.

A prominent aerodynamicist was having a conversation with a biologist. The biologist asked the aerodynamicist about the flight of bees. The engineer took a napkin, did a quick calculation on it and declared that based on the wingspan and size of the body of the bumblebee, it was impossible for the bumblebee to fly.

Similar to the bumblebee, when you try to move

out of your comfort zone of the nine-to-five job and want to embark on an unconventional way of earning a living, you may encounter people who say you can't. Or they may tell you not to move forward with your idea. The person telling you that you can't must first be qualified in order for their statement to be valid. The responsibility is on you to discern whether or not the suggestion is authentically intentional to work toward either the benefit or detriment of your idea.

The sad thing about your failings is that they will not come about because of scientists; they will come about because of family, friends and close associates. These latter people will not take a pen and work out on paper the odds of your failing. They will just use negative words to prevent you from exploring your possibilities. If you listen to them and succumb to their utterances of failure, you are doomed. Two words that have a devastating effect on the human psyche are *no* and *can't*. These two words are told to most children from an early age. Sadly, after the adults utter these words to young children, most of the time they give no explanations as to the reason for their saying *no* or *can't*.

From the time that we were little children, the sentences containing the aforementioned words that were frequently used on us by our parents and other family members were "No, you can't do that" or "No, you can't have that." These words are supposedly used by adults for the children's protection. But these words restrict the child's mind in the early stages of development. Most times, a child will retort, "But, Mom [or Dad], why can't I?" The parent will reply, "Because I said so!" Therefore, as adults, when we hear those words, they stifle our creativity and prevent us from developing our ideas that would otherwise move us forward in our adult lives.

The bumblebee, which does not know and cannot hear the words *no* and *can't*, goes ahead and does what is calculated by human beings to be impossible: it soars and proves the scientists wrong. We as human beings should adopt the bumblebee's attitude and make the impossible possible.

Henry Ford

One person who turned *no* and *can't* into *yes* and *I can* was Henry Ford. When he decided that he would build an automobile and stated his intentions, he was challenged and taken to court by some noted lawyers of the day. The lawyers argued that it was impossible for Mr. Ford to build an automobile because he only had a Grade 8 education; therefore, his capacity for thinking beyond his education was limited according to the judicial system.

The lawyers were in for the shock of their lives! Once Henry Ford entered the witness stand and was questioned by the lawyers as to his ability to build an automobile, he told the court that he didn't have to possess any knowledge or skill to build a car in order to be able to produce a finished product.

The judge asked Mr. Ford to expand on his statement. He continued: "All I need is to surround myself with people who can perform the various tasks. On my desks, there will be a series of 'electrical buttons' that lead to each department, and when I want to find out anything pertaining to the construction of the automobile, I just have to press the appropriate button. The head of that department will come to me, and any information that is required as it pertains to the manufacturing of the automobile [will be provided]." The case against Mr. Ford was thrown out of court because of his testimony. Can you imagine what would have happened to the human race if Henry Ford had lost the court case?

Our mode of transportation may have remained the horse-and-buggy.

Mr. Ford went ahead with his idea and built his first one-cylinder gasoline combustion engine in the kitchen of his house. This was in the year of 1893. The quadricycle, as pictured, was completed in 1896. It was built in a shed at the back of his house. It was so named because part of its construction consisted of four bicycle wheels.

From the humble beginnings of the one-cylinder engine to the first quadricycle, the appetite of the population for automobiles increased and the industry began to take shape. Thus, the four-cylinder engine was developed.

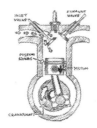

The one-cylinder engine.

The quadricycle.

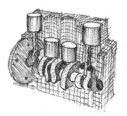

The four-cylinder engine.

I would suggest that one of Mr. Ford's reasons for success is that he did not entertain the thought of failing. Although Mr. Ford filed for bankruptcy several times, he saw an opportunity and said to himself, *I can!* And today, we can cast our thoughts on those tough times that Mr. Ford encountered; now, we have an admiration for the beautiful cars that we enjoy today because others have improved on Mr. Ford's early design. All we can do is thank Mr. Ford for staying the course until success was accomplished.

What about you? Will you stay the course, or will you abandon your dreams at the first sign of difficulty?

As reported by the United States Census Bureau, the world's population reached 7.7 billion people as of October 15, 2018. Of this number, approximately 4 billion people have not tapped into the trillions of dollars that are generated by the industrial apparatus of the industrial giants of the world. This can be seen in the Global Economic Pyramid, provided. It is therefore my aim to show that a need exists to help and inspire some of these people so that they, in turn, will come up with ideas. Some of the ideas will be acted upon, which will create jobs and products and services for the uplifting of humankind.

The Global Economic Pyramid

A total of 487 billionaires, including Bill Gates, are at the top of the Global Economic Pyramid.

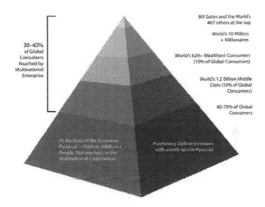

The people at the base of the Global Economic Pyramid need a *hand up*, not a *handout*! How can this be accomplished?

There is a large number of skilled baby boomers who would be happy, I think, to lend a helping hand to people in the so-called "Third World" countries by way of a transfer of skills. But who are the baby boomers? These are the people who were born between January 1, 1946, and December 31, 1964.

How did this large demographic of people come about? At the end of World War II, upon the troops' returning home from the battlefield, the men needed a lot of tender loving care; as a result, a lot of lovemaking occurred between the men who had fought in the war and their wives, resulting in a large number of babies being born in the subsequent years. As of January 1, 2011, the first baby boomer reached age 65. Since that time, every day, over 10,000 of these boomers have been turning age 65. It is reported that this trend will continue until the year 2029. This has the potential to cause major problems for governments. The resources that are required to facilitate this large group of people will be stretched to the limit and, quite possibly, be exhausted. But what can be done to ease the situation?

Swords to Ploughshares

The various factions of governments throughout the world could come together if they see this as an urgent matter, but they must have a sincere humane desire to do something about moving humankind to another level. How? They could set up a *global* skilled educational system and ask the skilled baby boomers from the developed world to help in the training of people from the developing world. This training should consist of two parts, one part being practical and the second part being theoretical, with the emphasis of the training placed on the practical area. Most people learn more by hands-on training. This is the reason why doing something as opposed to learning theory about it is stressed. There are also a large number of able-bodied retired people who would be happy to do a three- or six-month rotation in the various developing countries, participating in such worthy projects. This would be an example of fulfilling the prophecy written in the Bible, as stated in the book of Isaiah and Micah, of turning swords to ploughshares.

> They will beat their swords into ploughshares and their spears into pruning hooks.
> Nation will not take up sword against nation, nor will they train for war anymore. (Isa. 2:4; Mic. 4:3)

The struggling people of the world do not need

weapons! They need the basic necessities of life, starting with *food*. But first, they must have a *skill* in order to do work and to be able to purchase and grow food! This would allow them to manufacture products that would enable them to trade with the developed world.

Can you imagine how many novel ideas are sitting idle among the vast pool of people who are sitting at the bottom of the economic pyramid?

The idea of swords to ploughshares is a concept, but everything that is created starts with a concept. Think of the possibilities if humankind would gravitate toward the "sword to ploughshares" idea.

George Washington Carver

Let's look at another man of ideas. In the 1800s there was a man who initially lived at the bottom of the economic pyramid, and in spite of overwhelming obstacles that he encountered from his birth to adult life, he never lost sight of his idea.

This man is responsible for the agriculture that we enjoy today. His name was George Washington. This is not the George Washington who was the former president of the United States of America. This George Washington Carver was the food scientist who moved the farmers of the southern states from a cotton-growing mentality to a food-growing production solution.

Carver was stolen by slave traders when he was a baby and was prevented from learning to read and write by the government of the day. Still, he was privileged, later in life, to be invited to the White House in Washington, DC, to demonstrate his various agriculture products to the President of the United States of America and to Congress.

"George Washington Carver was born in Missouri on the Moses Carver plantation. His parents were slaves. His father died right before George was born, then while he was still a baby, slave traders kidnapped him and his mother. Only George was returned to the plantation." There was never a trace of George's mother again. One can only imagine how she died!

Carver began his formal education at the age of 12 because of segregation of the black and white races of people at that time. He was forced to leave the home of his adopted parents and to move to Newton County in southwest Missouri, where he worked on a farm during the day and studied in a one-room schoolhouse at night. This would have been a clandestine affair because it was against the law to teach black people to read and write. If one were caught doing so, such person would be punished.

Later in life, as laws were being changed pertaining to black people, George Washington Carver attended Minneapolis High School in Kansas. Racial barriers were quite prevalent at that time, and as a result, upon completing high school, Carver found that college entrance was yet another obstacle. After being accepted to Highland University in Kansas, he was rejected when the governing body of the university discovered that he was black. Nevertheless, Carver held fast to his idea to become the best food scientist and decided that he was not going to let the roadblocks that were placed in his path prevent him from achieving his *goal*. "At the age of thirty, Carver gained acceptance to Simpson College in Indianola, Iowa, where he was the first black student."

As you read the following, you will realize the impact that George Washington Carver had on the farming industry and, even today, on the production of food.

George Washington Carver is perhaps one of the most famous names in U.S. history. People generally know him as the inventor of peanut butter, but his contributions to science go way beyond that.

As stated by P. J. Williams, "Peanuts, however, grew very quickly. Soon, the peanut crop threatened to overwhelm the farmers at Tuskegee. Carver came to the rescue by finding [use] for [peanuts]. He ultimately invented *more than 300 products that used peanuts* in their development; they include cheese, milk, facial cream, ink, shampoo, and soap, just to name a few."

As a result of solving problems, other problems may be initiated that may threaten to undermine the success of the initial problem. Such was the case with Carver's scientific application to the problem with the introduction of nitrate-rich soil. Carver's successful *idea* of creating nitrate-rich soil created a problem with the overproduction of peanuts. This problem had to be solved! The new scientific idea of nitrate-rich soil enhancement *led to* the development of over 300 additional peanut-related products, as has been stated above.

From unfavorable and perilous beginnings, George Washington Carver became one of the United States' greatest educators and agricultural researchers.

Among his many famous achievements at Tuskegee are these:

- "He taught his students and other agriculture experts the practice of rotating crops, to ensure that fields didn't wear out their nutrient potential.
- He directed the planting of peas, which took nitrogen from the air and transferred it to the soil, creating nitrate-rich soil that was perfect for planting cotton and tobacco.
- He did the same with peanuts, which were also successful in enriching the soil."

Can you imagine what our lives would be like today

if George Washington Carver's fate had been similar to that of his mother after they were stolen and had he not been returned to his slave master? What if Carver had quit in his attempt to obtain an education during his struggles?

George Washington Carver in his science lab at Tuskegee Institute, in Tuskegee, Alabama.

George Washington Carver, the world's greatest scientist.

I believe that every human being has a purpose in life. I am also of the opinion that the plan for our lives is mapped out for us long before we arrive here in a physical form. However, for us to live our lives to our full potential, we must find something that we love to do, and we must have a passion for it and work at it until we conquer the thing that was once only an idea. Today, because of Carver's unwavering faith and his zeal to help in the development of humankind, these beautiful words are inscribed on his tombstone, located at Tuskegee University, Alabama, USA:

"He could have added fortune to fame, but caring for neither, he found happiness and honor in being helpful to the world."

Procrastination

What do you have bottled up inside of you that needs to be *unleashed* so that your ideas can reach great heights? Other people have done it! Why not you? You must continue on your quest to succeed, and you may ultimately soar to heights similar to those reached by the bumblebee. How would you like your epitaph to read? Start now and work on your thoughts so as to change them into positive ideas. Don't live for yourself; live to serve others. This is the secret to your success.

It is said that the richest places on earth are graveyards. Why? Because a lot of people are placed in these final resting places who had ideas and talents that would have contributed to our pursuit of our development and would have allowed us to live more comfortable, more enjoyable lives while also helping others to succeed in their search for the basic necessities of life. Several factors may have prevented these deceased people from moving forward with their ideas. However, we will focus on one, *procrastination*, which is one of the major stumbling blocks that get in the way.

For example, I had an *idea* to create this book, with the hope that after having read it, you the reader would be motivated, stop procrastinating and take action to move toward your goal. The idea of my writing this book came to me approximately two years prior to my taking action; therefore, you may conclude that I *procrastinated* for a while! I will propose that procrastination is normal for the human being. However, while *procrastination* might be fine for a limited time, the problem is that too many of us never move forward. Our procrastination becomes a rut. One must make a conscious decision to move forward.

Nevertheless, procrastination ("I will do it tomorrow") prevents a large number of people from achieving their goals and developing their God-given talents and abilities. Tomorrow becomes weeks, weeks become months, months turn to years, old age approaches, aches and pains attack the body; these aches and pains occupy the brain, and then people spend most of their time lamenting of their ills and expressing remorse over what should have been. The heart stops, and their ideas and talents go to the graveyard with them. Can you identify with the aforementioned, or have you ever encountered someone who fits into this category?

I had a friend whom I will call Pat. She was a registered nurse and also a great cook. Quite often, she would invite me over to her house for Sunday dinner. After tasting the delicious cuisine that she had prepared, I would enquire as to the recipe that she'd used. The first time I asked Pat what the recipe consisted of and how she had prepared the food, she said, "I am not telling you just yet!" I considered her response to be a form of procrastination. Over the years I asked about her recipes at least six times. The response was always the same. I finally came to the realization that I was not going to receive her secret recipes. Nevertheless, I continued to enjoy her food whenever I was invited to her house for dinner.

One day, while Pat was walking along College

Street at the intersection with Yonge Street in Toronto, she suffered a massive heart attack and died. She took with her to the grave all of that knowledge about the food that she loved to cook. What good is that to me and others who could have benefited from Pat's recipes?

In reading about Pat's demise, one may say, "What is the big deal? It is only food!" No matter how insignificant our knowledge may seem, we must share it with others in order to develop our talents, because others may look at our project and give us some input for how we can improve the process or the design to enhance the final outcome. What if all human beings adopted an attitude similar to Pat's? Imagine if one person possessed all of the knowledge and decided not to share it with anyone else. If you are to move forward and help others, you must think outside the box. It is the only way anyone can assist in the development of humankind.

Thinking Outside the Box

To help in the pursuit of happiness, you must think and then share your thoughts and ideas with others. It is argued that people who have ideas and create things to help humankind are people who think outside the box. But what is this box that is referred to by individuals?

I would suggest that it is our educational system. Once they enter school, children are taught the alphabet, vowels and the numerical system, all of which are part of the school's curriculum. As a result, we literally function within these parameters. This system prepares us for a job when we leave school. Hence, it connotes that we are boxed in educationally.

As a teacher, I am not suggesting that the educational system is unnecessary. However, I am aware that there are essential components missing from the curriculum that are applicable to the development of one's entire life. For example, the curriculum does not include how to start a business or how to manage one's finances. This includes what to do with our first pay cheque and the ones we will receive upon our retirement.

It is a simple concept: You should pay yourself first, and this amount should be at least 10 percent of your earnings. This concept is explained in *The Richest Man in Babylon*.

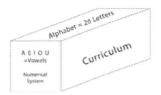

To work outside this box, one must think creatively and act on his or her idea.

If you were to employ your efforts with the latter (i.e. the 40/40 plan), your life would be less stressful where money is concerned. On the other hand, if you are still on the 40/40 plan, (working 8 hours a day for 5 days a week [for a total of 40 hours] for 40 years), you are still operating within "the box." There is nothing wrong about working within the box because it is not how much you earn; it is how much you save. For example, if a person is working for an average wage of $15 an hour for 40 hours, he or she will be paid $600. This is a week's pay. If he or she receives this amount for 52 weeks, the total amount earned will be $31,200 for the year. The employable years—40 years—at $31,200 per annum will generate $1,248,000. This is the person's lifetime earnings. The question I ask is why 95 percent of the population lives from pay cheque to pay cheque and dies broke after earning this large sum of money? (Tax deductions are, of course, not included in this equation.)

You may be thinking about this and asking yourself, *Can this be possible?* I want you to think about what I am going to propose at this time. Do you know of anyone, perhaps it's even you, who worked for a company for 10, 25, 30 or 40 years and then circumstances changed within the company? For example, the company downsized;

the owner decided to relocate the plant to Mexico; or the boss who liked you or that person suddenly left the company? The new boss arrived and decided to do some housecleaning, and you were, or that person was, one of the employees who got *axed* or, to make it more palatable, "made redundant."

While you were working you felt comfortable going to work and receiving a weekly or monthly pay cheque. But suddenly, you became very uncomfortable, knowing the pay cheque that you received weekly or monthly was no longer available because you'd been fired. Suddenly, you no longer had the comfort of that box to rely on. While you were working, you focused only on your wants and neglected your needs. What do I mean? You needed some place to live. But did you need that $4 Starbucks coffee every morning, or do you merely want it?

Ninety-five percent of the working population works within the comfort zone of the *box*. The previous diagram gives a visual representation of your thinking outside the box as related to working within the box. As a result, ideas can lead to action, which can lead to change and positive results.

You see, when a person works within the box, he or she obtains a linear income. The person exchanges his or her time for money. On the other hand, when a person comes up with an idea and implements the idea and it becomes a success, he or she receives a constant flow of money from that idea. This is called passive income, or residual income. This is similar to what Robert A. Chesebrough of New York, USA, did.

The Vaseline Story

Men working on the rigs drilling the oil wells for crude oil saw a sticky foreign substance appearing on the drills. The sticky substance caused the drills to freeze up. The men shared their observations of the sticky substance with others; if they had not shared what they saw with others, we may not be enjoying the use of Vaseline today. The following quote is to help you to realize the importance of sharing your thoughts, ideas and observations, as these can drastically enhance the lives of humankind. And in so doing, you, through this *selfish* act of sharing, can change the financial situations of other people.

"The Vaseline journey started in 1859 when a 22-year-old chemist from Brooklyn, New York named Robert A. Chesebrough went to Pennsylvania, to investigate an oil well. Chesebrough discovered a gooey substance known as 'Rod Wax' that was causing the oil rig workers problems. It would stick to the drilling rigs, causing them to seize up."

On one hand, the "rod wax" caused a problem with the operation of the drilling rigs, but on the other hand, the rod wax helped in the healing of the cuts and burns the oil workers received.

"Chesebrough observed that the oil workers would smear their skin with the substance that formed on the drills, as it seemed to aid the healing of burns and cuts of the workers' body." After further investigation and experimentation of the rod wax, Chesebrough was successful in extracting a usable product by the name of petroleum jelly, which we now know as Vaseline, from the rod wax.

Robert A. Chesebrough.

Chesebrough was born January 9, 1837, and lived until September 8, 1933. He was a chemist and the inventor of petroleum jelly (Vaseline). He founded his manufacturing company in 1875, and it became the leading company in the area of personal care products of which petroleum jelly is one of the main ingredients.

Today, Vaseline is a household name. The product is used on babies and adults throughout the world. This is an example of sharing an observation with another person. A word of caution, however. One has to be careful about whom one shares observations and ideas with. For example, you should not confide in a person who has a negative attitude, or with Uncle Bob who goes to the basement on Friday evenings after work and sits there, drinks beer and watches sports until Sunday night. Chesebrough's idea to explore the healing potential of rod wax resulted in a product that is used in many skin care products and other medical applications today. When one has an idea, one should act on it because one does not know what changes may come about as a result of taking such action.

In the psychology of human development, it is argued that human beings go through six stages of growth and development: Stage 1 is dependency. During stage 2, which occurs between the ages of 20 and 30, primary concerns are established—making money, making connections and competing for a place in society. Stage 3, which takes place between ages 30 and 35, concerns raising children and seeking approval from others. Stage 4, occurring from age 35 to age 45, is when one starts to question what is really important in life. At stage 5, between the ages of 45 and 65, people begin to fully comprehend and embrace their purpose of life. At stage 6, people have met many critical developmental milestones and are beyond any need for social approval. Based on the aforementioned, it can be argued that Mr. Chesebrough fits into stage 2. I would argue, however, that these findings may not hold true in every case. One should consider these stages in order to prepare for various stages that one may encounter to propel him or her forward in a positive way.

On the other hand, Colonel Sanders, who developed the recipe for Kentucky Fried Chicken, was reported to be 40 years old when he started his Kentucky Fried Chicken business. This was done on a very small scale. He then franchised the KFC business when he was 66 years of age. Therefore, Mr. Sanders combined two stages of development: stage 4 and stage 6.

60,000 Thoughts, 80 Percent of Them Negative

As you go through the various stages of development, you are bombarded with many thoughts and voices in your head. Most of them are negative. For example, your thoughts and doubts would say, *That is* impossible. *I* can't *do that. It is* too difficult. *Where am I going to get the money to start that business? Surely, the bank is not going to lend me any money because I am not* credible! The negative list gets bigger and longer as you get older.

But how do the negative thoughts that imbed themselves in one's psyche come into being? It can be argued that these come about as a result of one's surroundings and association of kinship. It is also argued that "a person is the average of his or her five closest friends"; therefore, if you are associated with five positive-thinking people, you will be more positive in your thinking and actions. The opposite is also true. Negative thoughts of your close associates will cause you to have mostly negative thoughts and tendencies.

Why do some human beings let their negative thoughts prevent them from developing their ideas? Neuroscientists believe that they have stumbled onto the root cause of some people's inaction.

Scientists have discovered that approximately 60,000 thoughts go through the human mind daily; out of the 60,000 thoughts, 80 percent are negative and only 20 percent are positive. The following chart and exercise is therefore designed to help you make some positive changes within your thinking, which ultimately will help you change your life for a more productive and rewarding future.

	#1	#2	#3
1			
2			
3			
4			

	#1	#2	#3
5			
6			
7			
8			
9			
10			

1) In the chart above, write down 10 things that are negatively affecting you and keeping you from accomplishing your goals and dreams in life.
2) Draw a single line through each of the things in column 1 that you have no control over or each of the things that appears to you to be an impossible task to accomplish. (In considering an example of an "impossible" task, please refer to the following story of Paul at the grave.)
3) Transfer the remaining things from column 1 to column 2.
4) Now in column 3, you are going to write out how you are going to remedy each problem in column 2, also providing a timeline of when you are going to solve each problem and a statement of how you will do so.

You may have to purchase a notepad to write your entries on in the event that you have more than 10 problems that you have to work on.

Note: If you do not complete the task of solving a given problem within the timeframe that you have chosen, you can adjust the date. However, you have to be specific about the second date and work on completing the task before that time. Otherwise, the task will become a futile experience, whereas its intention is to propel you forward through organizing positive thoughts for your development.

Paul at the Grave

There are different problems or similar problems that each of us will encounter in our lives. How we deal with these problems can dictate our happiness or misery in our day-to-day living. For example, you may know someone who, because of a disagreement, has not spoken to his or her father or mother for the last 10 or 20 years. During those years, this individual may have wanted to approach his or her dad or mom to talk to him or her so as to reconcile their differences. The person, as the master of procrastination, kept putting off approaching the parent. In the meantime, his or her dad or mom suffered a massive heart attack and died suddenly.

This affected the person to the extent that it bore negative results with his or her own spouse and job. The once beautiful relationship that existed between this married couple became an antagonistic affair. The person you know would leave home for work every day and, instead of going to work, would go to the cemetery, sit on his or her father or mother's grave, cry and talk to the father or mother with the expectation of hearing a voice coming from below with comforting words.

If this scenario were written in your first column, you would cross it out and *not* move it to the second column. This would be a *dead* situation (no pun intended), meaning that there is nothing to be done at this time to fix it. You will only be dealing with what you have control over now.

You may be thinking that no one would do what I

have just described. Well, consider Paul's story. Paul was a teacher, working at a large secondary school in the Greater Toronto Area. A problem existed between him and his father. Paul had never resolved the issue that tarnished the relationship between him and his dad. One day his dad suffered a heart attack and died. This devastated Paul to the extent that it prevented him from performing his duties at home and at work. Help was offered to him by the school board. He was removed from the classroom and placed in the administrative office. The school administrators thought that having Paul at the board office would prevent him from leaving work and going to his father's grave to sit, talk and cry, but he continued this practice.

The school board administrators made several attempts to help Paul, but all these attempts failed. He continued to visit the cemetery. Paul's wife could not cope with the stress any longer. As a result, she left him and took their beautiful daughter with her. Paul just could not understand that. As an employee, he exchanged his time for a pay cheque. If there was no time worked, there was no money earned! Eventually, the school board had no alternative but to part ways with Paul. He was terminated.

Reflection

At some point in time, life will throw you a curveball. How you handle that ball when it comes your way will dictate your future. The problems that you are working on become your daily blueprint for success. Please take notes of your progress daily. Remember—problems are a positive part of living. I suggest that they are placed in our lives so that we may learn from them and use them to grow to become better human beings if we so choose.

Every problem has a negative and a positive component attached to it; therefore, one must examine the problem and take from it the part that is beneficial to one's success. Every living human being has encountered a problem or problems of some sort. Right now, as you read this text, you are having a problem, solving a problem or entering into a problem. If you have never experienced a problem, have no fear: a problem of some kind is on its way!

Let us examine some of the problems that others have encountered when attempting to implement the ideas that have brought us to the standard of living that some of us enjoy at present.

Proverbs 29:18

After Henry Ford's success with manufacturing the four-cylinder engine, there was a need for an engine that was capable of producing more power. As better roads were constructed, more power was required under the hood. Mr. Ford had an idea of designing an eight-cylinder engine. Ford was a visionary; he had the ability to gaze (or look) into the future. This is referred to as having vision. What does this mean? The majority of people have sight, but only a select number of people have vision. It is this latter group of people who come up with ideas that change the world, resulting in a better lifestyle for human beings.

Proverbs 29:18 of the Bible states, "Without vision, the people perish." There are a select few who are given the special gift of vision. Anyone who is fortunate in receiving this special gift can see things before they become reality. Ford was one of these individuals. Mr. Ford visualized the changes that would result from designing an eight-cylinder engine.

Ford assembled his engineers and instructed them to design and build an eight-cylinder engine. After several months of trials, no success was seen. The engineers told Mr. Ford that the task was impossible. Ford instructed his engineers to stay on the job until success was achieved, no matter how much time was required. He gave the engineers an ultimatum: "Produce an eight-cylinder engine, or be fired!"

As stated in the introduction of this book, ideas create fortunes and help to move this world forward. But a job provides us a living. Ford threatened the engineers' livelihood. This caused them to give the project 100 percent of their effort.

The eight-cylinder crankshaft.

This was the key to the eight-cylinder engine that the engineers designed after months of trials.

That effort of the engineers produced the key that was required in the development of the eight-cylinder engine that previously was missing. The engineers struggled and agonized as they sought to develop the product envisioned by Mr. Ford. They did this for what to them must have seemed like a lifetime.

Six months later, the engineers returned to Ford to inform him that they had succeeded in designing the eight-cylinder engine. How had they come up with the idea to accomplish the task that was given to them by Mr. Ford?

I would suggest that when the human lifeline is threatened, people will develop their God-given talents and abilities to prevent a disaster from destroying their way of life. You see, the thought of being fired was the motivating factor for the engineers to solve the problem. They designed a crankshaft (see the image "The eight-cylinder crankshaft") that would allow two connecting rods to be attached to one crankshaft journal. This allowed the manufacturing and casting of two, four-cylinder engine blocks to be cast as one unit, set side by side in a *V* formation.

The *V* engine block   Crankshaft   Connecting Rods

The components shown in the illustration are the engine block, the crankshaft and connecting rods. The two connecting rods are connected to one journal. This allows two rods to be connected to one journal for two pistons to operate on the left and right side of the engine at the same time.

The idea of a V-8 engine became a reality. The idea, once developed into a product, greatly improved the industrial sector of the United States and quickly spread to other parts of the world. Larger engines could now be built to handle the ever increasing power needs of engines that required for boats, trains, planes, lorries (trucks) and other motorized vehicles that are now necessary to aid in the building of societies throughout the world.

Garrett Morgan

As new ideas are fostered and systems are implemented, they can sometimes create problems. And because of the new problems, other ideas are formed in the human psyche.

The creation of the automobile caused a traffic problem. The number of vehicles increased. Drivers in the towns and rural communities, when approaching intersections, did not know who had the right-of-way.

Garrett Augustus Morgan was an African-American inventor and a successful businessman. Born March 4, 1877, Morgan was the child of former slaves. He was the seventh child of eleven in his family. "He only acquired an elementary education;" but that did not stop him from succeeding in his business ventures. Because of Garrett Morgan's successful business adventures, he acquired enough money to purchase an automobile.

Driving along the streets of Cleveland one day, Garrett realized that he was also part of the problem. The car that he was operating created an unsafe situation with other vehicles at intersections. An idea was formed in Garrett's mind; he was determined to make driving safer. He wanted to be part of the solution, not part of the problem.

Because of Morgan's foresight of a looming traffic problem, he patented a traffic signal on November 20, 1923 (U.S. patent no. 1,475,024). This was the first traffic signal patented, but it was not the first invented. Morgan's traffic signal was a T-shaped pole with arms (but with no lights) that had three signs, one or more of which popped out at different times: a red "stop," a green "go," and another red "stop in all directions." This last signal indicated to pedestrians that it was safe to cross the street. "It was controlled by an electric clock mechanism." This device became very popular and was used all around the USA. "Morgan sold his device to the General Electric Corporation for $40,000 [a huge sum of money at that time]. His device was used until the three-light traffic signal was developed." If you have a burning desire to succeed, then neither education nor which side of the tracks you were born on can hinder you.

Morgan was the first person to patent a traffic signal.

He also developed the gas mask (among many other inventions).

Some of his inventions included such devices as a safety hood and smoke protector for firefighters (patent no. 1,113,675, in 1912) and, aforementioned, the gas mask (patent no. 1,090,936, in 1914). He also developed a zigzag sewing machine attachment, a hair straightener, hair dying lotions, and decurling hair combs. Today, the decurling hair comb is called the curling iron (patent no. 2,763,281, in 1956). These were only a few of Garrett's successes until his death on August 27, 1963.

Garrett A. Morgan, traffic signal.

I have presented you with three individuals who, as a result of their tenacious drive, moved us forward in our pursuit of happiness and comfort. But these people did not let the lack of education stand in their way on the path to greatness. If they had stayed in the mode of thinking inside the box, instead of thinking outside the box, our lives as we know them at present would be quite different.

Say you worked at a company for many years and were quite comfortable with your job. But at retirement, what can you take home with you? You may be given a farewell party, a speech delivered by the boss full of well-wishes, and a token of appreciation. *Well*, is that all that you were worth? You gave the company the best years of your life, only to be thrown out as trash and given a gift valued at no more than $50. Imagine that!

So as to avoid this type of fate, you should start thinking differently. You must think of ideas and implement them so as to change the course of your financial trajectory and your children's—and their children's—legacy.

Can being too ambitious and wanting to climb the corporate ladder cost you the job you loved and worked at for 20 years? If so, would you let that hold you back from moving forward?

Clarence Saunders

Let me introduce you to how your favourite supermarket, where you now stand in line waiting to check out, came about. There was a young student who dropped out of school and was in search of a job in order to provide for his daily living necessities such as food, clothing and shelter. He lived in Memphis, Tennessee, USA, and his name was Clarence Saunders. He obtained his first job at a grocery store. When he started this job, packing boxes and groceries at age 14, having quit school, he was excited and full of enthusiasm. Can you recall how you felt when you got your first job? Sometimes I relive the experience of obtaining my first job. And as I look back to those years, I sometimes wonder where that feeling of elation that was present then has gone. I can empathize with Saunders when approaching the shopkeeper (his new boss) and offering suggestions as to how he could make the grocery store more efficient.

One day Clarence Saunders saw a group of people waiting in a line at a self-service establishment and an idea popped into his head of how a similar system could be implemented at the grocery store he was working at. Upon arriving at the grocery store for his next shift, and without hesitation, Clarence approached his boss and told him that he could weigh and prepackage the groceries, place them on shelves in aisles and have the customers walk through the aisles and serve themselves. His boss listened. When Saunders finished explaining the idea, his boss said, "I hired you to unpack boxes and pack groceries. I did not hire you to *think*. The next time you come to me with any crazy *ideas*, I will fire you!"

Can you imagine how a 14-year-old person would feel after having his boss threaten to fire him because he'd shared what seemed to be an excellent idea of progress? Nevertheless, Saunders continued working at the grocery store unpacking boxes and packing groceries, simultaneously working on his idea. Saunders decided that he was not going to be constrained by anyone on his journey to success. He continued to work on the idea that his boss had chastised him for.

When the time was right, Saunders ventured out and implemented his idea. Because of Saunders's vision and persistence, his success can be seen worldwide today. He started the first self-service supermarket in Memphis, Tennessee, on September 6, 1916. It was called the Piggly Wiggly.

Today, a replica of the original Piggly Wiggly is located in the Pink Palace Museum and Planetarium in Memphis, Tennessee. The illustration shows the a replica of the world's first supermarket.

Clarence
Sunders

The First Piggly Wiggly
Supermarket

This is a more up-to-date store built after Saunders had had his original idea. Today, supermarkets can be seen all over the world.

This is a modern version of a Piggly Wiggly supermarket.

It all started with one simple idea of a 14-year-old school dropout!

Unlike Saunders, when some people are confronted with challenges pertaining to their employment, they recoil and are afraid to move forward. I will introduce you to Marg, who handled her situation in a different way. Marg is a pseudonym used to protect her identity.

I live in Mississauga, Ontario. In the mornings, I usually go for a power exercise walk at around 6:00. After my power walk, I stop at Second Cup Coffee Shop for a small cup of strong coffee. The coffee shop is located on the southeast corner of Eglinton Avenue and Hurontario Street. On one of my morning visits to the coffee shop, I encountered a woman with whom I started a conversation. After the initial meeting, we became conventional buddies. As a result, we would talk with each other every morning about various topics. During our conversations, I discovered that she worked in the medical field and had been employed with her present employer for 20 years.

On one occasion, I stopped at the coffee shop around 2:00 p.m. To my surprise, I saw Marg in the far corner, tucked away with four large books. She was in deep concentration with one of the books.

I was reluctant to disturb her, but she motioned to me that I should come over. As we were talking, she told me that she was studying to apply for a higher position at her workplace, which would ultimately pay her more money. She also said that she was somewhat nervous because her final exam was within two weeks and she had not written an exam in a very long time. I gave her a few pointers on how she should prepare for the exam. I introduced her to the "cone of learning." This is a graph that shows how learning is retained, based on one's senses. She thanked me. I wished her good luck on her exam and left her to her studies.

Four weeks passed without my seeing Marg, as I'd had to leave the country on business. I returned within four weeks and started my morning routine of taking walks. I stopped at the coffee shop, and there she was, smiling!

As we were talking, she told me that she had passed the exam and had applied for the higher position at work. I was delighted to hear of her success and wished her well in her new endeavors.

One morning of the following week, I saw her at the coffee shop. She had a sad look on her face. I enquired as to what was making her sad. She was reluctant to tell me. After my probing, she finally told me that she had not gotten the new position; what she received instead was a *pink slip. She'd been terminated from her job.* Marg was bitter, with a negative attitude toward her boss and the company. As time wore on, she was unable to let go and move on with living her life. I introduced her to some of the people who had suffered disappointments during their lifetimes, such as Saunders and Edison. I hope she explored the readings I suggested and used those people's setbacks as inspiration to make her own comeback. Every setback we encounter during our journey in life is just a pause for a comeback. However, most people hold the pause button and never let go of it or move forward with their ideas. I am unaware of Marg's current whereabouts, but it is my hope that she took my suggestions and acted on them to propel her forward in her endeavors.

Thomas Edison

Most of us are confronted on a daily basis with ideas, much like Saunders, but only a few of us ever take action. We hear of people who accomplished what may seem to be difficult tasks; however, most people never stop to think about or to investigate the road traveled by those who went before us. If we were to investigate their accomplishments, it may inspire some of us to initiate the process to implementing the idea or ideas that we have been mulling over for a long period of time.

Thomas Edison.

When the name Thomas Edison is mentioned, the first things that come to mind are electricity and the incandescent light bulb. But most people are not aware of Edison's invention of a machine to capture and replay sound. When Edison had the idea of recording sound, he made a drawing of what he envisioned to accomplish the task of recording sound and then playing back what had been recorded. He called his model maker into his office, handed him the drawing and instructed him to produce a finished operational product based on the drawing. The model maker took one look at the drawing and said, "Impossible!" Mr. Edison asked why he thought that it was impossible. The model maker replied, "Because no one has ever made a machine that could talk." Edison told the model maker to go ahead and build the machine and "let me [Edison] be the loser." To the model maker's surprise, the recording machine worked on the first attempt once it was completed.

Sometimes during our journey in life, we may encounter some people who don't seem to acquiesce to what society considers as being the norm of interacting with others. For example, we may come across people who constantly question others, seeking to know more about various things, or people who seem aloof.

Because most people who are looking from the outside cannot comprehend what is taking place internally with another person, this can sometimes lead to criticism and labeling. This can be quite upsetting to the individual who is labeled and to members of his or her family.

Thomas Edison was the recipient of such name-calling and labeling. Edison was an inquisitive child, and because of his wanting to know more about how things worked and the science behind them, he constantly questioned his teacher, Reverend Engle. This irritated his teacher.

Edison's mind often wandered, and his teacher, Reverend Engle, was often overheard calling the boy "addled." When Edison's mother heard of this, she immediately removed her son from school, following a heated argument with his teacher.

The first time that I heard the word *addled* used, I was approximately 6 years of age. My parents kept hens for laying eggs and also for eating. Sometimes a hen would hide in the grass, lay her eggs and sit on them until the chicks hatched. When the little chicks were strong enough to walk, I would see a procession of several chickens behind the hen as she brought them out for display.

I would then search to see where the hen had hid, to surprise us with the beautiful little chickens. In locating the nest, I would find broken eggshells that had housed the chickens during their incubation period. Invariably, I would find an egg that was not broken. I recall the first occasion of my finding an egg, taking it to my grandmother and inquiring as to why the egg was still whole. She replied that it was "addled." Being a curious 6-year-old, I wanted to see what was inside the egg. I broke the egg while my grandmother was trying to say, "Don't!" I will never forget the yellow stuff that came out of the egg and the nauseating stench that seemed to linger for days.

Reading about Edison and his teacher's saying that he was addled brings to the forefront of my mind my early encounter with an "addled" egg, and what the word *addled* connotes. It is something that is rotten and of no value.

Sometimes one can take a negative situation and turn it into a positive life-changing event. This is exactly what Thomas Edison's mother did. Because of his teacher's "addled" comment, his mother, being a teacher herself, homeschooled Thomas and exposed him to books written by great thinkers about the course of history, such as Edward Gibbon's *Rise and Fall of the Roman Empire* and *The World Dictionary of Science*. Edison became interested in science, and this led to his scientific inventions—thanks to his parents, who did not let someone else's opinion decided the destiny and legacy of their son. What if his mother had bought into her son's ill-informed teacher's opinion? We would probably be using the kerosene lamp for light and would not be able to enjoy the renditions of musical legends long after they have left the physical earth.

Most human beings have opinions about others. Sometimes when opinions are cast upon individuals, these opinions are not always in the receiving person's best interests. Therefore, when an opinion is given about you, you must evaluate what has been said and ascertain if the person who is giving his or her opinion is qualified to be determining whether what you are doing has merit. In any event, the final decision must rest with the recipient. Before acting on a given opinion, you should figure out if the person has an ulterior motive. But in any case, the final decision rests with you, the decision maker. If you hear negative opinions about what you are planning to do, you must have a *gut feeling* that what you are about to undertake is going to work in your favour. A situation that comes to mind is that of James B. Duke (the name associated with Duke University).

Sometime during the business pursuits of James B. Duke, he came upon an old friend who operated two tobacco shops. Duke shared with the old friend that he intended to open two thousand tobacco stores across the United States. His friend, quite taken aback, replied, "My partner and I have enough trouble with just two stores, and you're thinking of opening two thousand. It's a mistake, Duke!" Duke went ahead with his idea and opened a chain of tobacco stores that would eventually gross millions of dollars weekly. Because of the wealth that Duke amassed, a result of the revenue from his tobacco stores, millions of dollars from his fortune were used to build Duke University. What if Duke had harkened to his friend's unfavorable position about Duke's idea?

Never let someone's opinion of you or what you are about to undertake be a hindrance to your success.

Elijah McCoy

When a person invents a product, invariably someone will copy the invention and pass it off as the original. This takes place with several accessories, including wristwatches and shoes, and with other household items, among other things. Therefore, when Elijah McCoy invented the oil-drip cup to lubricate the wheel bearings of trains, his product was referred to as "the real McCoy." It is said that the railroad operators did not want to install inferior copies of the oil-drip cup on the trains, and as a result, the engineers would request the "real McCoy" of the product when purchasing the cup. This made the copying of the product by imitators practically impossible.

Before the invention of the oil-drip cup, trains traveling across Canada and the United States of America would have to make frequent stops to have the wheel bearings manually lubricated by the engineers. This made train travel very time-consuming. After the invention and installation of the oil-drip cup, the time it took to travel by train was drastically reduced. The bearings were now lubricated automatically. Now, trains could travel from point A to point B without having to stop. Seeing the implementation and the success of the oil-drip cup on trains and the subsequent increase of revenue for the railroad companies, the owners of manufacturing industries in North America and across the world were encouraged to incorporate the automatic oil-drip cup system into their manufacturing equipment. This greatly improved operation and production of the manufacturing industry because the previously required downtime of the equipment for purposes of manual lubrication was eliminated. This one simple idea, implemented by a struggling Elijah McCoy, revolutionized the production of the world, and today we are enjoying the fruits of the "real McCoy."

But who was Elijah McCoy? He was born in Colchester, Ontario, Canada, in 1844, free from slavery, to parents who fled from slavery in the United States. After completing his formal education, he was sent to Scotland to study engineering because he had a zest for this line of work. After completing his engineering studies in Scotland, he returned to Canada. Unfortunately or fortunately, he was unable to obtain an engineering job. The only job that he could secure was that of a fireman on steam engine trains. His job was to keep the fire burning in order to produce steam to power the train engine. It was as he performed this grueling labour that the idea of designing the automatic oil-drip cup came to him. Would he have designed the oil-drip cup if he had obtained an engineering job? Or was it that he was working in an area not of his calling that forced him to see the need for improving the transportation of the railway system? It can be argued that McCoy took a negative position in his life and turned it into a positive situation that has helped to change the lives of countless people in this world.

Elijah McCoy

Martha Berry and Henry Ford

Life will give you any achievement that you desire only if you ask for what you want and apply yourself to the pursuit of it. For example, there was once a secondary schoolteacher who dedicated her life to uplifting the lives of the people who lived in the northern hills of Georgia in the United States. Her name was Martha Berry.

Ms. Berry.

Ms. Berry was born October 7, 1865, and became a schoolteacher who needed some money to keep a school operating that she had started for children who lived in the hills of northern Georgia. The parents of these children were financially strapped and were unable to pay for their children's education in the mainstream educational system.

Ms. Berry was in search of funds in order to operate the school. At the time of her search, Henry Ford had become successful in the manufacturing and distribution of the automobile. Martha decided to ask Mr. Ford for some financial help. After she'd made several unsuccessful attempts and tried to secure a meeting with Mr. Ford, finally he decided to meet with her.

During the meeting with Mr. Ford, Martha told him about her wanting to educate the poor children living in the hills. She asked Mr. Ford for some financial assistance, and he refused! But little did he know, Martha had a plan B in place, just in case her plan A failed, which it did. A plan B is like having a spare tire in the trunk of your car. You may not expect to have a flat tire, but in case you do, the situation can easily be taken care of. And you can proceed on your journey after replacing the defective tire.

Ms. Berry thanked Mr. Ford for meeting with her. As she was leaving, she turned around and made a request of Mr. Ford that was hard for him to refuse but which he found profoundly amusing. She asked, "Do you have any spare change that you can give me so that I can buy a bushel of peanuts for the children?"

Henry Ford, amused at Ms. Berry's request, pushed his hands in his pockets, pulled out some change and gave it to her. Can you imagine what was going through Mr. Ford's mind when Martha asked for peanuts? (*I refused her the big request, and now she is asking for peanuts.*) He found it difficult to deny the schoolchildren some peanuts. As he gave her the money, he probably thought, *This woman is crazy. Those peanuts will only last her a day or two as she distributes them among the schoolchildren. I am glad that I did not grant her the first request, because she would've only wasted my money on peanuts!*

Ms. Berry thanked Mr. Ford for the small change

and left. What Mr. Ford didn't know was that Martha had worked out a plan B before meeting with him, and it had worked beautifully. She purchased the bushel of peanuts, and she and the students of her school planted the peanuts, harvested the crop, sold the nuts, and sowed more peanuts and harvested them, all the while saving the profits that were earned. This procedure continued until Ms. Berry had amassed a large sum of money from this skillful venture.

Having the large sum of money that Ms. Berry had accumulated as the result of Mr. Ford's small gesture, she wanted to thank him. Martha sought another meeting with Mr. Ford. He probably thought that she wanted some more small change, so he met with her. However, what took place during the meeting between them set the school on a firm financial footing and ensured its place in history books. It also cemented a lasting friendship between Ms. Berry and Mr. Ford. Mr. Ford was named as the person to look after her legal affairs.

Martha Berry said to Mr. Ford, "I want to thank you for the money you gave toward the bushel of peanuts." She showed Mr. Ford the large sum of money that she and the schoolchildren had accumulated as a result of the small change he had given her. During this second meeting, Mr. Ford realized that it was not about money, but about what a person can do with it to help others. Mr. Ford then donated millions of dollars and farming equipment to the school, which placed it in a strong financial position.

Mr. Ford continued to support the school and gave millions of dollars, which provided for the construction of some magnificent buildings that are today still standing on the school's campus.

Martha could have followed the footsteps of her five sisters who had gotten married and embarked upon a different journey in life. But Martha opted for a different road in her quest that left a lasting legacy, that of helping others.

Martha died on February 27, 1942. Today the school that Martha started has been replaced by Berry College.

This just goes to show how one person's idea can change the world, leaving a legacy that will grow exponentially. I would argue that several people are called to provide valuable service that can help humankind; however, only a few heed the calling. The people presented in this book are just a few among that special group. There are, however, many more who have assisted in humankind's pursuit for a better life.

Closing

When I was a boy, I was fascinated with the bumblebee. I would cut small holes in matchboxes, catch a bumblebee, place it in the empty box and poke at it (in a gentle way) just to hear it hum. After the bumblebee got tired of my constant interference, it would cease to hum. I would release it and catch a different bumblebee.

I was warned by my parents that I was "playing with fire." This was the term they would use when I was approaching imminent danger. However, as a playful boy, I could not see the danger in playing with a bumblebee. My method of capturing the bumblebee was to use a folded piece of cloth. On one occasion, I attempted to catch a bumblebee and my parents' "fire" prediction was realized. It appears that the cloth I had used to capture the bee did not give the protection needed to protect my hand from the bumblebee. And yes, you guessed it! The bumblebee stung me, and I released it immediately. An excruciating pain traveled up my right arm. I was overcome with fear. From that day forward, anytime I saw a bumblebee cross-pollinating the flowers, I would just watch in amazement.

Because of scientific research, we know that the bumblebee performs a function important to the survival of human life. Bumblebees pollinate the flowers to provide food for the bees and their colony and to allow the plants to grow that provide food for us. It appears the spiritual force responsible for our existence gave specific scientific instinctual instructions to the bumblebee. The bumblebee continues to amaze scientists with its ability to fly. It follows its instinct, doing what it must do on a daily basis. On the other hand, it is reported that in Genesis God gave Adam and Eve simple instructions.

> Adam and Eve lived in the Garden of Eden. God and Jesus came and talked to them. There were many trees in the garden. God said Adam and Eve could eat fruit from all the trees but one. (Gen. 3:8; 2:16–17)

When we examine the bumblebee's purpose for being here on earth among us, we find a clear reason for their existence. But what is our purpose for being here on earth? Yes, some of us go to work daily to provide food and shelter, but aren't we more complex than the bumblebee? Why can't we focus on doing good deeds for others and help our fellow humans instead of trying to destroy each other? Are we in the quandary we're in because our forebears disobeyed the simple instructions that were given in the beginning?

There is no need for anyone living in this world to go from day to day without the basic necessities for human existence, such as an education, food, clothing, shelter, healthcare, and love.

I would suggest that most people who have acquired the basic necessities and have them in abundance and refuse to help the less fortunate do not really understand why we are here on earth.

I will argue that we are here because of the Supreme Being. You may call him by the name that your religious doctrine espouses, but for simplicity's sake, I will call him God.

> And God said, Let us make man in our image, after our likeness: and let them have dominion over the fish of the sea, and over the fowl of the air, and over the cattle, and over all the earth, and over every creeping thing that creeps on the earth. (Gen. 1:26)

The word *dominion* means control, power, authority, dominance and any other word that conjures up dominance. Therefore, when we look around the world and we see the chaos, we might argue that we have broken the number one rule that was given to us by the Creator. We as human beings are bent on controlling each other by force or by any other means that we can think of. Why? I would suggest that we do so for selfish reasons. The aforementioned Bible quote does not suggest that we should control each other!

Human beings are made up of great thinking stuff that is placed in the universe by the Creator. And we are given the ability to think and create things in order to live a comfortable and harmonious life while we are in a physical form here on earth. This is the reason that we as human beings were able to move from our cave dwellings and come to have this standard of living that some of us enjoy and even take for granted, referring to it as "living the *good life*."

How is it possible that we used and continue to use the thinking power that the Creator has given us to visualize and create all the things that we see around us and throughout the world? We are given the ability by the Creator to use our minds to tap into the formless matter of the universe to come up with ideas to form physical things for the benefit of humankind. *Just pause for a moment* and look around and ask yourself, how did all of the things we see and use on a daily basis *come* into being? Take for example the chair that you may be sitting on at this moment; or this book that you are reading now; or the car that you have parked in your garage or driveway. At one point in time, these things that are part of our daily lives did not exist.

An idea entered someone's mind; it was processed by the thought apparatus; it was then transferred to the hands and fingers in order to take on the physical form that is visible at present. *Please reread this chapter several times and have it fixed in your mind.* This could change your circumstance and help you to focus on your goals and dreams to reach a successful conclusion.

Throughout this book, I have given you examples of ordinary people who took ideas and brought them into reality. When are you going to let go of the 80 percent of the 60,000 thoughts that go through your mind daily that are negative, as argued by social scientists? Free your mind of the grudges, hate, resentments, greed, lust, lies, dislikes, prejudices and downright disdain that take up residence there, and live to help others. If you do, the next time you are asked what your purpose is for being here on earth, you will have the answer. It will be as simple as that of the bumblebee.

Based on your surroundings and all the negative influences that you encounter during your life's journey, you are not supposed to succeed in life. You will only eke out a meager existence in life. This is based on societal norms. Unlike the bumblebee, you can hear and articulate the negative voices that surround you daily. Because of these voices, you give up on life and perform tasks that will only supply your basic needs.

I don't know what stage in life you currently occupy. Regardless, if you are not happy with your present circumstances and want to change your direction, you can do so by focusing on the strengths you may have and start working on the goal that you have been thinking about for many years. Now that you have read this book and have been inspired by the encounters, you must stop procrastinating and move into action. Remember—success can be accomplished and measured in many areas of life. It only takes one person to initiate the process, as you have discovered by reading this book. Now, it is up to you to take the torch and run with it.

"If it is to be, it is up to me [you]." You must now place the idea that you have been thinking about for several years on paper and bring it into physical form. You will then become like the *bumblebee*. You will soar to great heights, similar to the bee. Why? Because you will have said that you *can*, and you will have gone ahead with your plan. Your family and friends will be amazed at your *success*!

Each day, our goal is to touch another's heart, to encourage another's mind and to inspire another's soul.

May you continually be blessed and be a blessing to others.

Acknowledgments

Throughout your journey in life, you will meet people of different beliefs and faiths. Some of them will help you, and some of them will set up roadblocks in your path with the hope that you will stumble, fall and fail. Make sure that you look up if you should fall. Because if you are face down, you will only have a restricted view of the pavement. On the other hand, if you look up, the beauty of the world abounds. You will be inspired to get up, brush yourself off and continue on your journey to success.

You have to be thankful for the encounters with both types of people mentioned above, because using your analytical skills, you can gain from the good experiences and also the bad experiences you bump into along the way.

I am thankful for all the positive people whom I have encountered along my life's journey. Special thanks goes to my uncle Fred. I used him as my role model. I am grateful for the help and direction I received from him along my path to success.

And all those people who attempted to derail my progress and success along life's journey, I thank them too. I have come to the realization that when so-called friends, partners and associates deliberately set you up in life's journey for a fall, it is only a pause for you to regroup and make a comeback. Handling these unpleasant situations well allows you to set your sails of life in the right direction to allow the wind of success to carry you on your journey.

Most of all, I thank the spiritual force who governs this universe for guiding me with soft voices and for directing my path when I was tempted to take the rough road of life.

Also, special thanks goes to my son Galen for providing the artwork for this book.

References

Africa and the Cinema.

Best, Wilfred D. *The Students' Companion.* London: Longman, 1991.

Bloom, A. *The Republic of Plato.* 2016.

Brown, L. *12 Laws That Turn Dreams into Reality.* 2017.

Clason, G. S. *The Richest Man in Babylon.* 1926.

Guide to Investing.

Hill, N. *Laws of Success.* 1925.

———. *Think and Grow Rich.* 1987.

———. *A Year of Growing Rich: 52 Steps to Achieving Life's Rewards.* 1993.

Howard, V. A., and J. H. Barton. *Thinking on Paper.* 1988.

Johnson, S. *Who Moved My Cheese?* 2000.

Sparke, C. *Entrepreneur Success Recipe.* 2012.

Schumand, H. *A Course in Miracles.* 1976.

Smith, E. *37 Things Every Black Man Needs to Know.* 1991.

Virgil, R. Fitzgerald, trans. *The Aeneid of Virgil*. 1990.

Welsing, F. C. *The Isis Papers: The Keys to the Colors*. 2004.

Williams, J. C., R. Dempsey, and M. Multhaup. *What Works for Women at Work*. 2014.

Williams, M., and A. Henry.

Williams, P. J. *The Alchemy of Race and Rights: Black Scientists and Inventors*. 1991.

About the Author

Tyrone Ward is a retired high school teacher. Born in Barbados, he spent a number of years living in England and in Texas, and now he resides in Canada. He is the father of four and has two teenage grandsons.

During his teaching career, he realized that more is required in the educational system. Students graduating from school should have a skill in addition to mastery of the basic curriculum.

This sparked the idea to create a collection of motivational short documentaries for students and others in the hope that they will choose to act upon their ideas no matter the circumstance, with the possibility of further shaping this world.

Printed in the United States
By Bookmasters